REAL WORLD DATA

GRAPHING WEATHER AND CLIMATE

Chris Oxlade

www.heinemann.co.uk/library
Visit our website to find out more information about **Heinemann Library** books.

To order:
☎ Phone 44 (0) 1865 888066
🗎 Send a fax to 44 (0) 1865 314091
 Visit the Heinemann Bookshop at www.heinemann.co.uk/library to browse our catalogue and order online.

Heinemann Library is an imprint of Pearson Education Limited, a company incorporated in England and Wales having its registered office at Edinburgh Gate, Harlow, Essex, CM20 2JE – Registered company number: 00872828
Heinemann Library is a registered trademark of Pearson Education Limited
Text © Pearson Education Ltd 2009
First published in hardback in 2009
First published in paperback in 2009
The moral rights of the proprietor have been asserted.

All rights reserved. No part of this publication may be reproduced in any form or by any means (including photocopying or storing it in any medium by electronic means and whether or not transiently or incidentally to some other use of this publication) without the written permission of the copyright owner, except in accordance with the provisions of the Copyright, Designs and Patents Act 1988 or under the terms of a licence issued by the Copyright Licensing Agency, Saffron House, 6–10 Kirby Street, London EC1N 8TS (www.cla.co.uk). Applications for the copyright owner's written permission should be addressed to the publisher.

Edited by Nancy Dickmann, Rachel Howells, and Sian Smith
Designed by Victoria Bevan and Geoff Ward
Illustrated by Geoff Ward
Picture Research by Mica Brancic and Elaine Willis
Originated by Modern Age
Printed and bound in China by Leo Paper Group

13-digit ISBN 978 0 431 02951 1 (hardback)
13 12 11 10 09
10 9 8 7 6 5 4 3 2 1

13-digit ISBN 978 0 431 02964 1 (paperback)
13 12 11 10 09
10 9 8 7 6 5 4 3 2 1

British Library Cataloguing in Publication Data
Oxlade, Chris
 Graphing weather and climate. - (Real world data)
 551.5'0728

A full catalogue record for this book is available from the British Library.

Acknowledgements
The publishers would like to thank the following for permission to reproduce photographs:
© Alamy pp.**6** (John Rensten), **8** (Emil Pozar), **13** (BKWine.com, Per Karlsson), **15** (© NASA); © Corbis pp.**4** (zefa, Herbert Kehrer), **10** (zefa, Leonard Lenz), **11** (Craig Aurness), **18** (Jim Reed), **19** (Eric Nguyen), **20** (Dabid Muench), **25** (Danny Lehman), **27** (Mike Theiss); © PA Archive (PA Photos) p.**17**

Cover photograph reproduced with permission of ©Getty Images (Taxi).

Every effort has been made to contact copyright holders of any material reproduced in this book. Any omissions will be rectified in subsequent printings if notice is given to the publishers.

The publishers would like to thank Harold Pratt for his assistance in the preparation of this book.

Disclaimer
All the Internet addresses (URLs) given in this book were valid at time of going to press. However, due to the dynamic nature of the Internet, some addresses may have changed, or sites may have changed or ceased to exist since publication. While the author and publishers regret any inconvenience this may cause readers, no responsibility for any such changes can be accepted by either the author or the publishers. It is recommended that adults supervise children on the Internet.

Contents

Weather and climate 4

Air, heat, and pressure 6

Winds 8

Clouds 10

Rain, snow, and hail 12

Weather fronts 14

Weather forecasting 16

Extreme weather 18

Climates 20

Seasons 22

Changing climates 24

The challenge of climate change 26

Chart smarts 28

Glossary 30

Further information 31

Index 32

Some words are printed in bold, **like this**. You can find out what they mean by looking in the glossary, on page 30.

Weather and climate

Did you make any decisions today because of the weather? Perhaps you took an umbrella, or put on sun cream, flew a kite, or went to the beach. Sunshine, clouds, wind, rain, and the temperature make up the weather at a particular time. The weather can be very different one day to the next, and even change from hour to hour.

 Weather is important for farmers. Crops need rain and sunshine to grow.

What is climate?

Does the weather change as the year goes by where you live? Perhaps it's cool, often cloudy, and windy with rain during one part of the year, but warm, often with sunshine, during another part of the year. This pattern is called a **climate**. Weather happens every hour and every day, but climate is a pattern of weather that happens over a long period.

Measuring the weather

Meteorologists (scientists who study the weather) measure and record the weather regularly. They measure temperature, wind, rainfall, and so on. The measurements show them what weather is happening at the time, which they need to make weather **forecasts**. The records show them what the weather was like in the past.

Weather graphs and charts

Meteorologists have to handle a huge amount of **data** from weather-measuring instruments. Graphs and charts made using the data help them to see patterns in the weather at a glance. A bar chart shows the amount of something or how often something happens. This graph shows how many hours of sunshine there were at a place each day for a week.

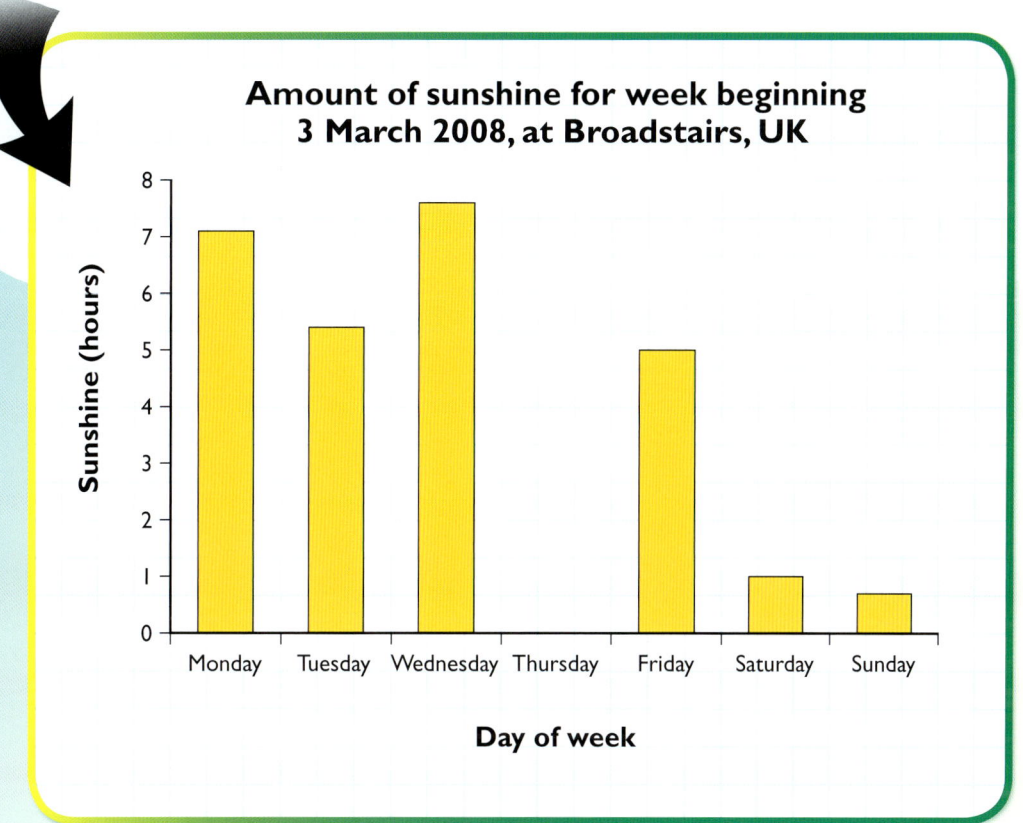

Air, heat, and pressure

The Earth is surrounded by a blanket of air called the **atmosphere**. The atmosphere is a few hundred kilometres thick, but all our weather happens in the lowest layer of air in the atmosphere, which is about 10 kilometres (6 miles) deep. The air in the atmosphere is made up of a mixture of gases. It is mostly nitrogen and oxygen, with a tiny amount of many other gases, including carbon dioxide. There is also normally some **water vapour** in the air (water vapour is the gas form of water).

Air pressure

The air in the atmosphere presses on everything in it, including you, although you don't notice the push. This push is called **atmospheric pressure**. It is measured in kilopascals or **millibars**. At sea level, it is normally between 98 and 104 kilopascals. We measure atmospheric pressure with a **barometer**.

 This barometer shows what sort of weather is likely to come as air pressure goes up and down.

Heating the air

Heat rays from the sun shine through the atmosphere and hit the Earth's surface. Some heat bounces off the surface and some soaks in. Where heat goes in, it makes the surface warm. Heat then flows from the surface into the air above, making the air near the surface warm. We measure the temperature of the air using a thermometer. Warm air tends to rise into the atmosphere, creating areas of low atmospheric pressure. Cool air tends to sink down through the atmosphere, creating areas of high atmospheric pressure.

Line graphs

A line graph shows how one thing changes with another. This line graph has a vertical axis (called the **y-axis**) which shows temperature. The horizontal axis (called the **x-axis**) shows time. The graph shows how the temperature changed at a place over 24 hours.

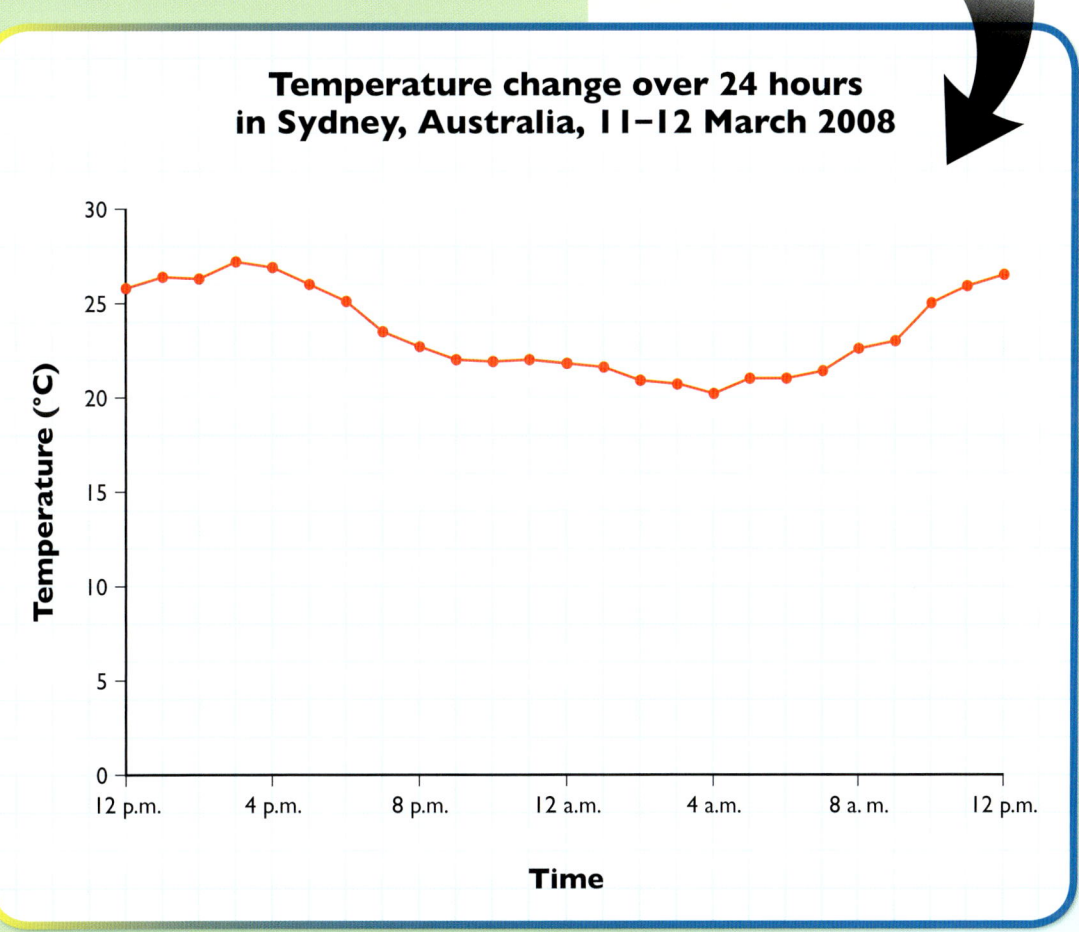

Winds

Wind is simply air moving from one place to another. Air always flows from where the pressure is high to where it is low. You can see this when air rushes from a balloon. The balloon squeezes the air inside, making the pressure higher inside the balloon than outside. The difference in pressure makes the air rush out.

Measuring winds

Meteorologists measure the speed and direction of winds. They measure the speed in kilometres per hour (kph) or miles per hour (mph), using an instrument called an anemometer. They measure the wind direction as the point on a compass where the wind is blowing from, using a wind vane.

Local winds

Differences in air temperatures often creates local winds. For example, at the coast, temperature differences set up winds called sea breezes. On a warm day, the land heats up more than the sea. The air over the land warms up and rises, creating low pressure. Cooler air from over the sea flows into the low pressure area. This forms a breeze that blows in from the sea.

 This shows an anemometer (right) and a wind vane (left). The anemometer spins when the wind blows.

Global winds

Temperature differences across the world cause regular winds that blow across oceans and continents. For example, the area around the **equator** (the tropics) is heated more than areas to the north or south. Air over the tropics rises, creating low pressure. Air flows in from the north and south, creating winds known as the trade winds. Further from the equator, winds known as westerlies and polar easterlies are created.

A special bar chart

This type of chart is used on marine charts for sailors. It shows them which way the wind blows most often (which is called the prevailing wind). It is like a bar chart bent into a circle. This chart shows how many days in a month the wind blew from different directions at a place. The longest arrow shows the direction from which the wind blew on the largest number of days.

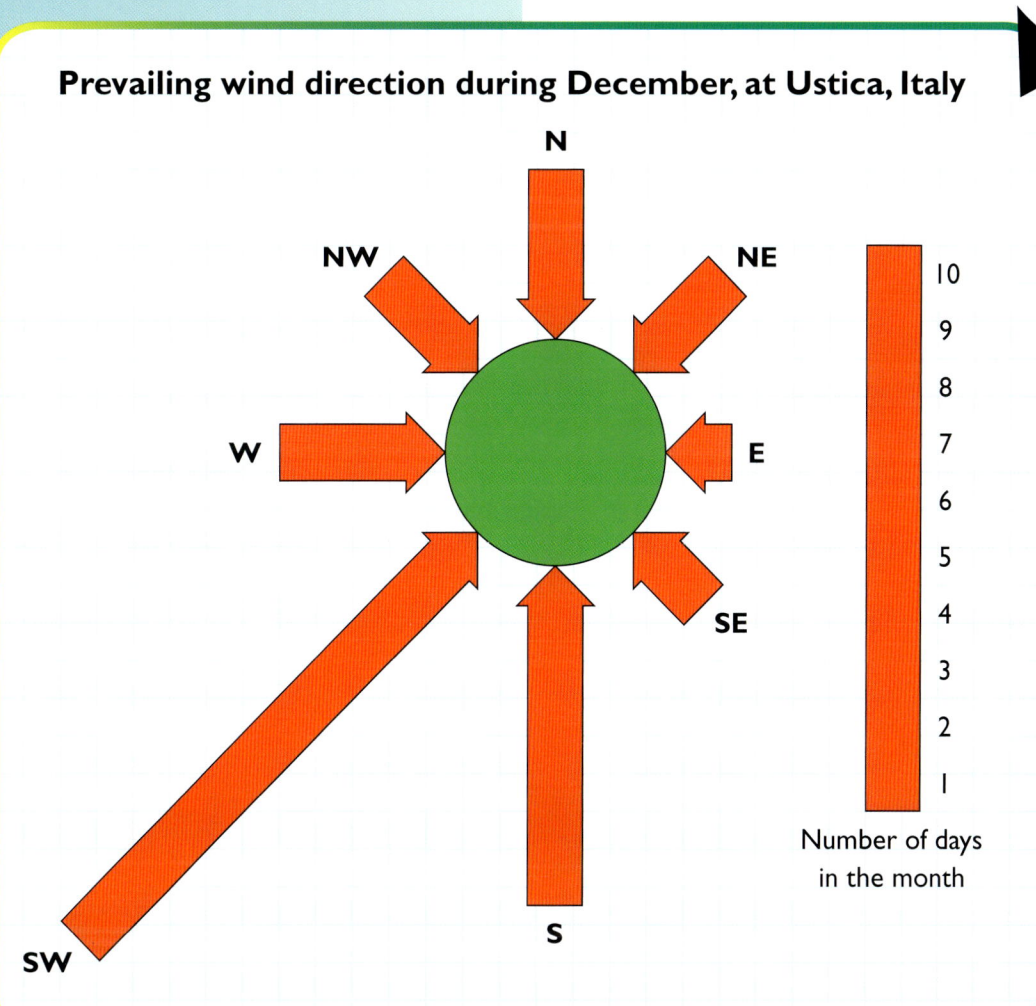

Prevailing wind direction during December, at Ustica, Italy

Number of days in the month

Clouds

Water exists in three forms (states), which are ice, liquid water, and **water vapour**. There is normally some water vapour in the air, but you can't see it. The water vapour forms when liquid water in the oceans, lakes, and ground **evaporates**. The amount of water vapour in the air is known as **humidity**. When there is lots of water vapour in the air, we say that it is humid, and the air feels warm and sticky. We measure humidity with an instrument called a **hygrometer**.

Forming clouds

When air that contains water vapour cools, the water vapour turns back to liquid water. It forms tiny drops of water. If the air is very cold, the water vapour turns to ice instead of water drops, forming ice crystals. Clouds are made up of millions and millions of water drops or ice crystals swirling about in the air. Most of the large clouds we see form when air rises upwards, which makes it cool.

 These are cumulus clouds. They formed when humid air rose upwards and cooled, which made water vapour turn to tiny water droplets.

Cloud names

Meteorologists have names for the many different shapes and sizes of clouds. The names come from words in Latin that describe the cloud shapes. There are two main types of cloud, cumuliform and stratiform. Cumuliform clouds are puffy, heaped clouds, and stratiform clouds are flat, layered clouds. Cloud names also tell us how high in the **atmosphere** the clouds are. Cirrus means the clouds are high-level clouds, and alto means the clouds are at middle level. For example, altostratus clouds are middle-level layered clouds.

 Meteorologists call enormous thunder clouds like these cumulonimbus clouds.

Pictograms

A pictogram shows the amount of something using pictures. This pictogram shows how much of the sky was covered by cloud during an afternoon. No shaded clouds would mean a clear sky. Five shaded clouds would mean complete cloud cover.

Cloud cover over an afternoon

Time	Cloud cover
12 noon	☁
1.00 p.m.	☁ ☁ ☁
2.00 p.m.	☁ ☁ ☁ ☁
3.00 p.m.	☁ ☁ ☁ ☁ ☁
4.00 p.m.	☁ ☁ ☁
5.00 p.m.	☁

No cloud cover — Complete cloud cover

Rain, snow, and hail

Water is constantly moving between the oceans, the **atmosphere**, and the land, where it soaks into the ground, is taken up by plants, flows down rivers, and collects in lakes. This movement is known as the **water cycle**. The water **evaporates** from the oceans and from the land and forms clouds. Any water or ice that falls from clouds is called **precipitation**. It can be rain, snow, or hail. When it lands, it soaks into the ground or flows down rivers back to the sea, and the cycle starts again.

 The movement of water between the oceans, the atmosphere, and the land is called the water cycle.

Drops and crystals

When clouds first form, the water drops or ice crystals are extremely tiny. Swirling air currents carry them around and around in the cloud. But gradually water droplets collide and join together, forming larger droplets, and ice crystals grow larger. Eventually the drops or crystals become heavy enough to fall from the cloud. Ice crystals normally melt as they fall through warm air under a cloud, forming rain. But if the air is cold enough, they fall to the ground as snow. Hail forms when water droplets go up and down over and over again in powerful air currents in thunder clouds, gaining layers of ice.

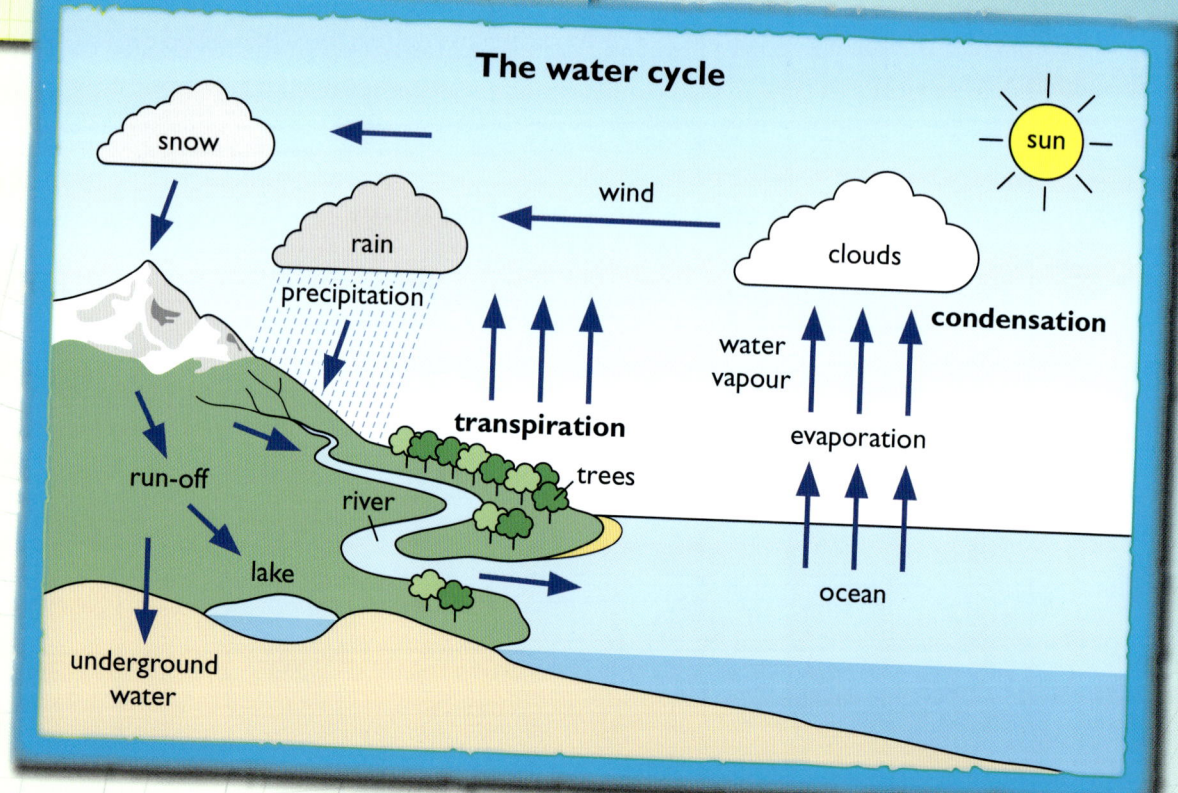

Measuring rainfall

Rainfall is measured in millimetres. We measure rainfall with an instrument called a rain gauge. The rain falls into a collecting funnel and runs down into a narrow collecting container. The narrow neck of the funnel stops the rain evaporating before it can be measured.

Double bar charts

This bar chart compares rainfall at a place in two different weeks. This sort of chart is called a double bar chart. The key tells you what **data** the different coloured bars refer to. In this case, the blue bars are for one week, and the red bars are for the following week.

 On this simple plastic rain gauge, the scale down the side shows how many millimetres of rain have fallen.

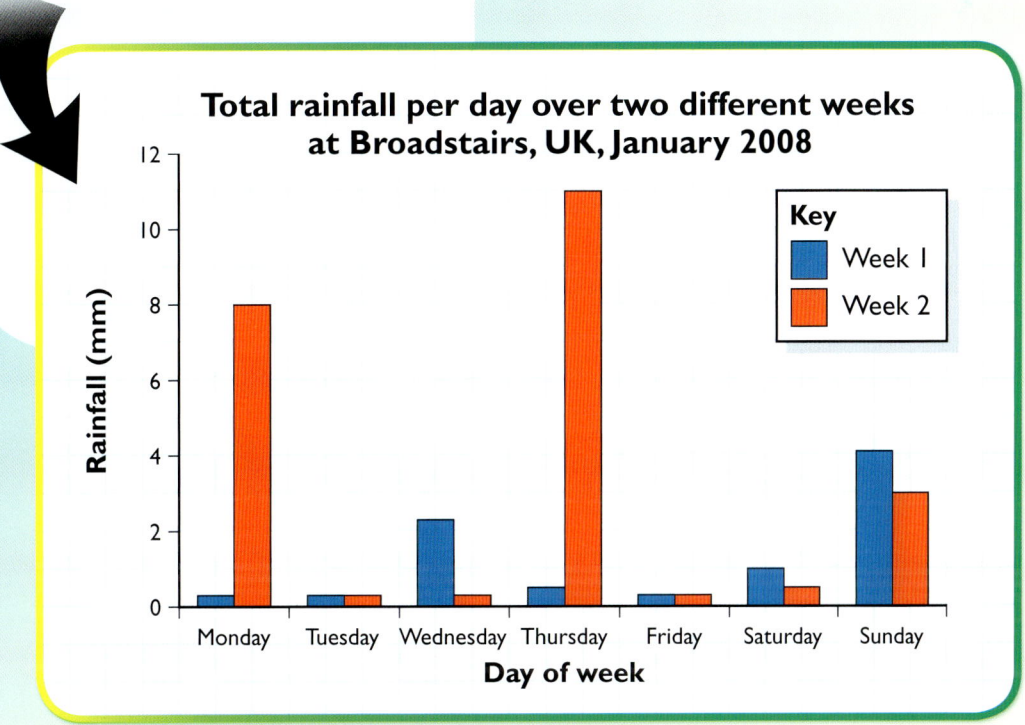

Weather fronts

The sun heats different parts of the Earth by different amounts. In turn, the Earth heats the air in the **atmosphere** by different amounts. This creates huge bodies of air at different temperatures, which **meteorologists** call air masses. Where two air masses meet, the boundary between them is called a weather **front**.

Warm fronts

When a warm air mass moves towards a cold air mass, the boundary between the two masses is called a warm front. On the ground, cold air is replaced by warm air as the front passes by. The warm air is less dense than the colder air, and it rises slowly over the cold air. As it does, **water vapour** in it turns to cloud. As a warm front approaches, you see high, wispy cirrus cloud, then layers of lower cloud, which may bring rain.

 These diagrams show how warm and cold weather fronts form.

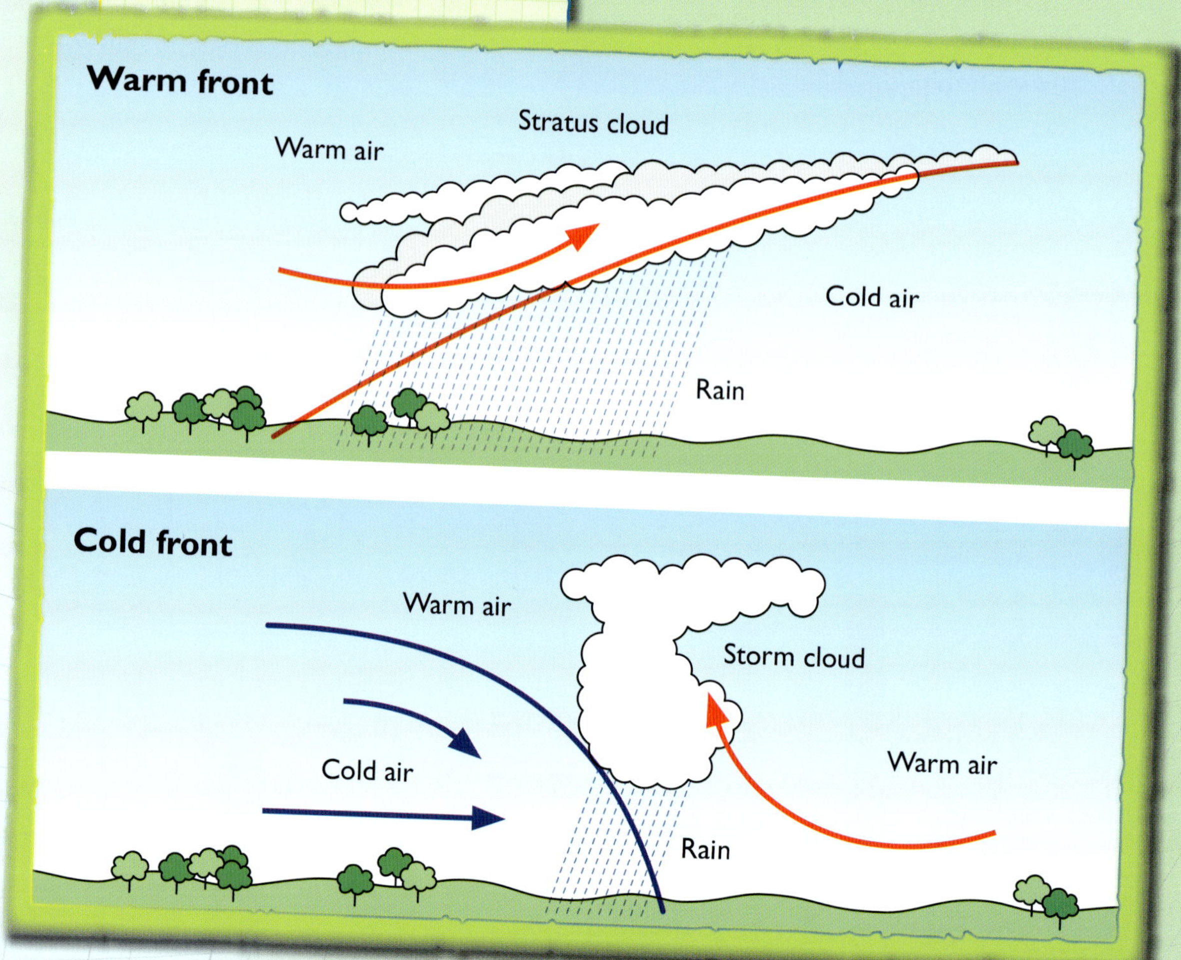

 This **satellite** photograph shows a low-pressure system south of Australia. Winds are blowing clockwise around it.

Cold fronts

When a cold air mass moves towards a warm air mass, the boundary between the two is called a cold front. On the ground, warm air is replaced by cold air as the front passes by. The cold air is more dense than the warm air, and it pushes under the warm air, forcing it upwards. The warm air rises and cools quickly, and cumulus clouds or stormy cumulonimbus clouds form. As a cold front approaches, you see large cumulus clouds, which bring heavy rain or snow, and strong winds.

Weather systems

Where large masses of warm air and cold air meet, parts of the front between them can begin to rotate around each other. This creates a large spinning weather system, called a low-pressure system, or low. Low-pressure systems bring unsettled weather, with rain and strong winds. There are also high-pressure weather systems. These do not contain fronts. They bring settled or fair weather.

Weather forecasting

Weather forecasting is predicting what the weather will be like over the next few hours or next few days. **Forecasts** are vital for some people. For example, sailors and pilots need forecasts to plan safe journeys, and farmers need forecasts to decide when to harvest crops.

Weather observations

In order to make a forecast for the future, **meteorologists** must know what's happening now. They measure the weather at observing sites, where there are collections of measuring instruments such as rain gauges, **barometers**, and thermometers. These sites are on land and on rigs and buoys at sea; some are manned and some are automatic. Meteorologists also rely on remote sensing devices. **Radar** tells them where rain is falling, and photographs from **satellites** show them how weather systems are developing and moving.

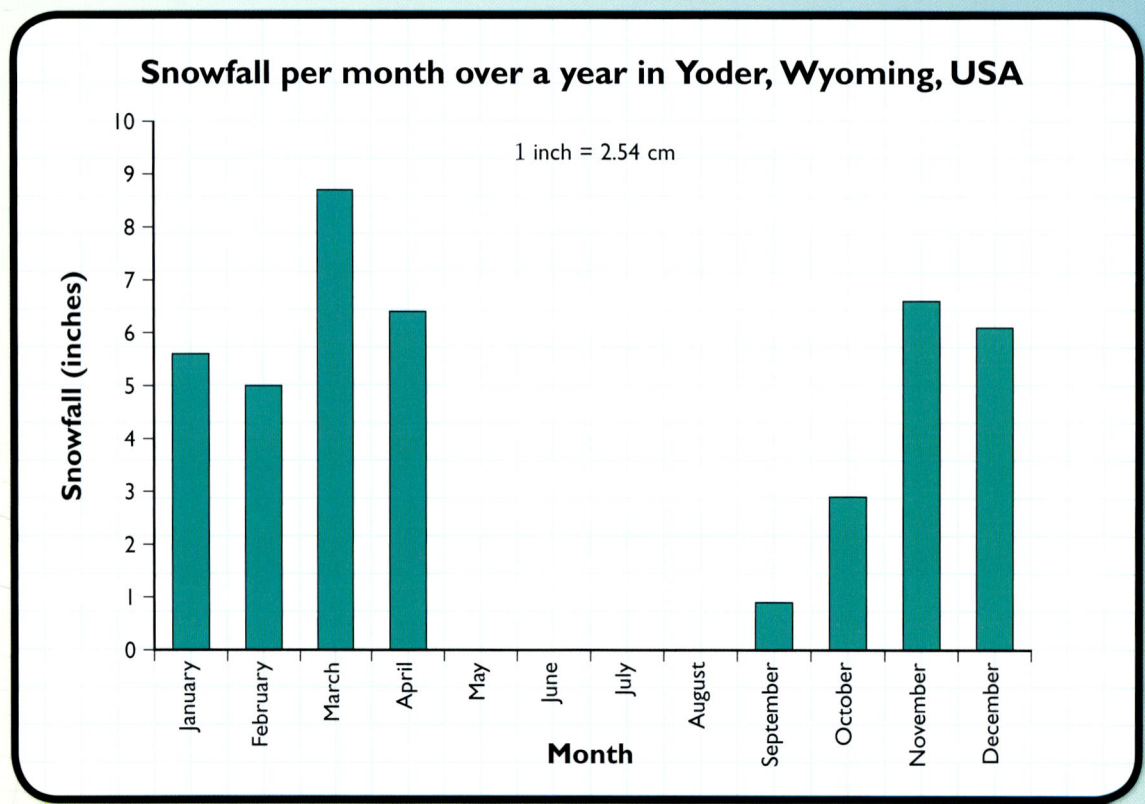

 This is a bar chart of snowfall over a year. Records like this help forecasters to see the months when snow is likely to fall.

Making forecasts

The **data** from observations is fed into complex computer programs called models, which run on some of the most powerful computers in the world. The models analyse the data and predict what will happen to the weather over the next hours and days. Weather forecasters study these predictions, along with data from radar stations and satellites, and then make their forecasts.

Severe weather warnings

When forecasters think there is a threat of severe weather, such as strong winds that could damage buildings, heavy rain that could lead to floods, heavy snowfall, or **tornadoes**, they give out a severe weather warning. These warnings allow people to prepare for the severe weather, move indoors, get off the roads, or even evacuate their homes.

 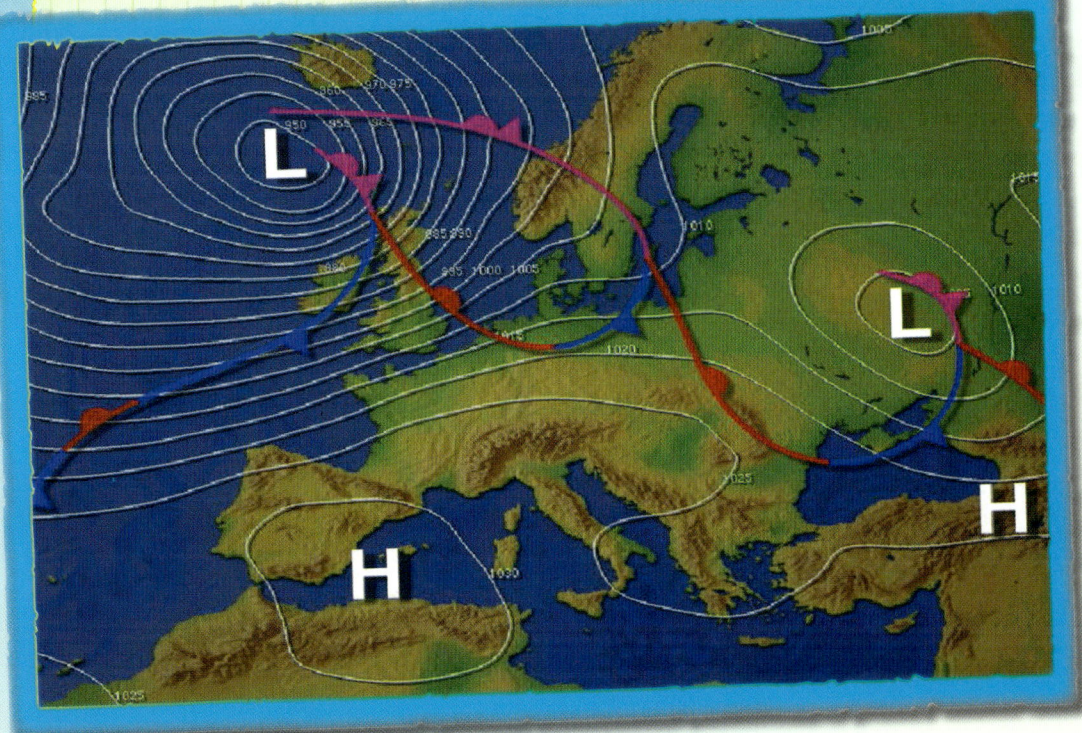

This weather map shows high-pressure (H) and low-pressure systems (L), and weather **fronts** (in colour). The white lines (isobars) join up places where pressure is the same.

Extreme weather

Extreme weather includes very strong winds, very heavy rain, snow, or hail, and very high or very low temperatures. Extreme weather often happens in remote areas, such as mountains, in the Arctic and Antarctic, and in deserts. But sometimes it happens in places where many people live, and here it can be very dangerous.

Extreme precipitation

Heavy rain is not harmful itself, but its effects can be deadly. Extremely heavy rain falling for just a few hours causes flash floods and mudslides. Days of rain over a large area makes rivers flood. Lack of rain is also a problem. It causes **droughts**, which stop crops growing.

Extreme temperatures

When the temperature at a place is much hotter than normal for a few days or more, we say that there is a heatwave. Where people are not used to high temperatures, they can become ill or even die from overheating. Long periods of very cold weather make it difficult for people to keep warm.

 Giant hailstones that fell on Nebraska, USA. Hailstones like this have injured and killed people.

Tropical cyclones

A **tropical** cyclone is a swirling weather system many kilometres wide that brings strong winds and heavy rain. **Hurricane** is the name for a tropical cyclone in the Atlantic Ocean. If a tropical cyclone hits land, its winds damage buildings and its rain causes floods. It also causes powerful waves and a rise in sea level (called a **storm surge**) that can flood low-lying coasts.

Tornadoes

A **tornado** is a spinning funnel of air, usually only a few hundred metres across, that comes down from a giant thunder cloud. Inside the funnel, winds can reach speeds of 300 miles (500 kilometres) per hour. These winds rip buildings apart, pick up cars, and hurl wreckage about.

 This tornado ripped apart houses in Kansas, USA, in 2004. Kansas is in an area of the United States called Tornado Alley.

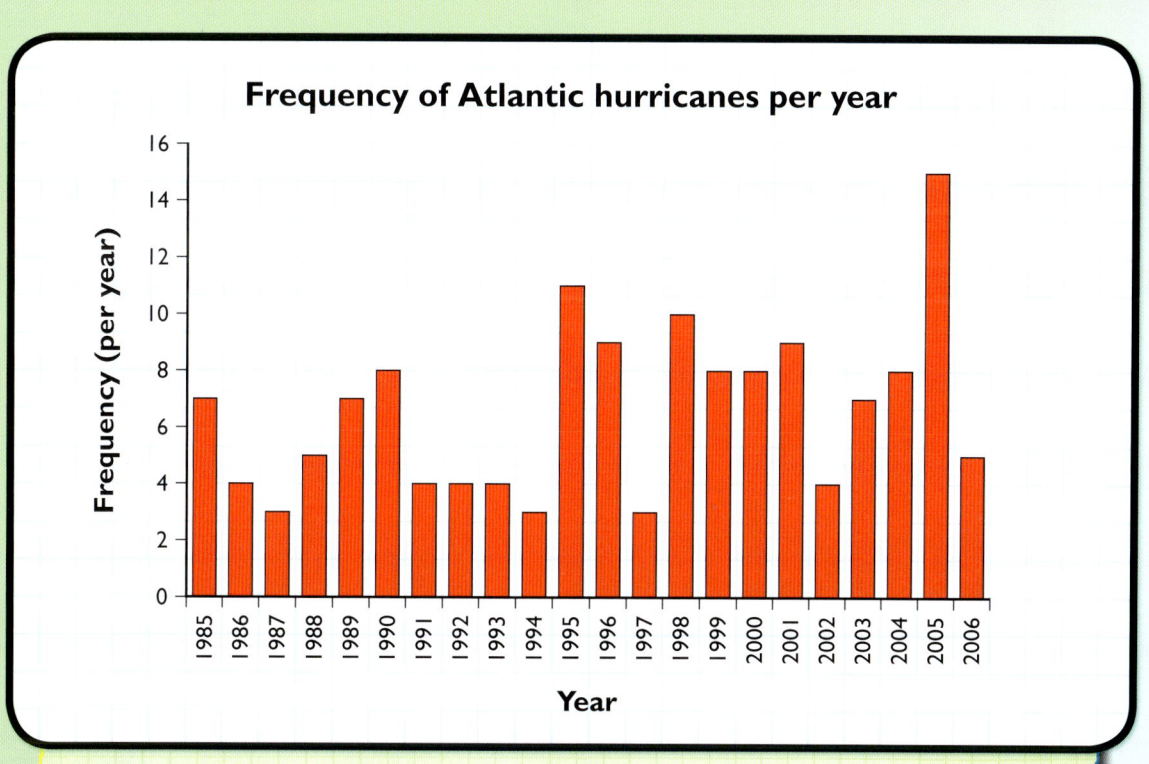

 This chart shows the number of hurricanes in the Atlantic each year.

Climates

The **climate** of a place on the Earth is the pattern of weather that happens there over a long period of time. It is not the same as the weather that happens from day to day. For example, in a place with a **tropical** climate, it is warm and humid all year round, with lots of rainfall. The pattern of weather normally repeats itself each year.

Measuring climates

To work out the climate of a place, **meteorologists** look at weather records for the place for 30 years or more. They work out the average weather that happens as a year goes by. They use many years of **data** because the weather in a place is never exactly the same every year. A year will always be hotter or colder, or wetter or drier than the year before.

World climates

Different areas of the world have different climates. For example, in a place with a polar climate, it is cold all year round, and there is not much **precipitation**. In a place with a **temperate** climate, there are warm periods (summers) and cool periods (winters), and some rain all year round. In a place with a desert climate there is hardly any rain all year round.

 Plants, such as cacti, that live in desert climates are adapted to survive on tiny amounts of water.

Local climates

Mountains, seas and oceans, and cities all affect climate. For example, a place on one side of a mountain range can get less rain than places a few kilometres away on the other side. And the climate in a city is often slightly warmer than in the surrounding countryside. These local climates are also called microclimates.

Comparing information

These charts compare the temperature and rainfall at places with two different climates, one tropical and one temperate. Rainfall is shown in a bar chart because rainfall is an amount, measured from zero. Temperature is shown in a line graph because it can be negative as well as positive.

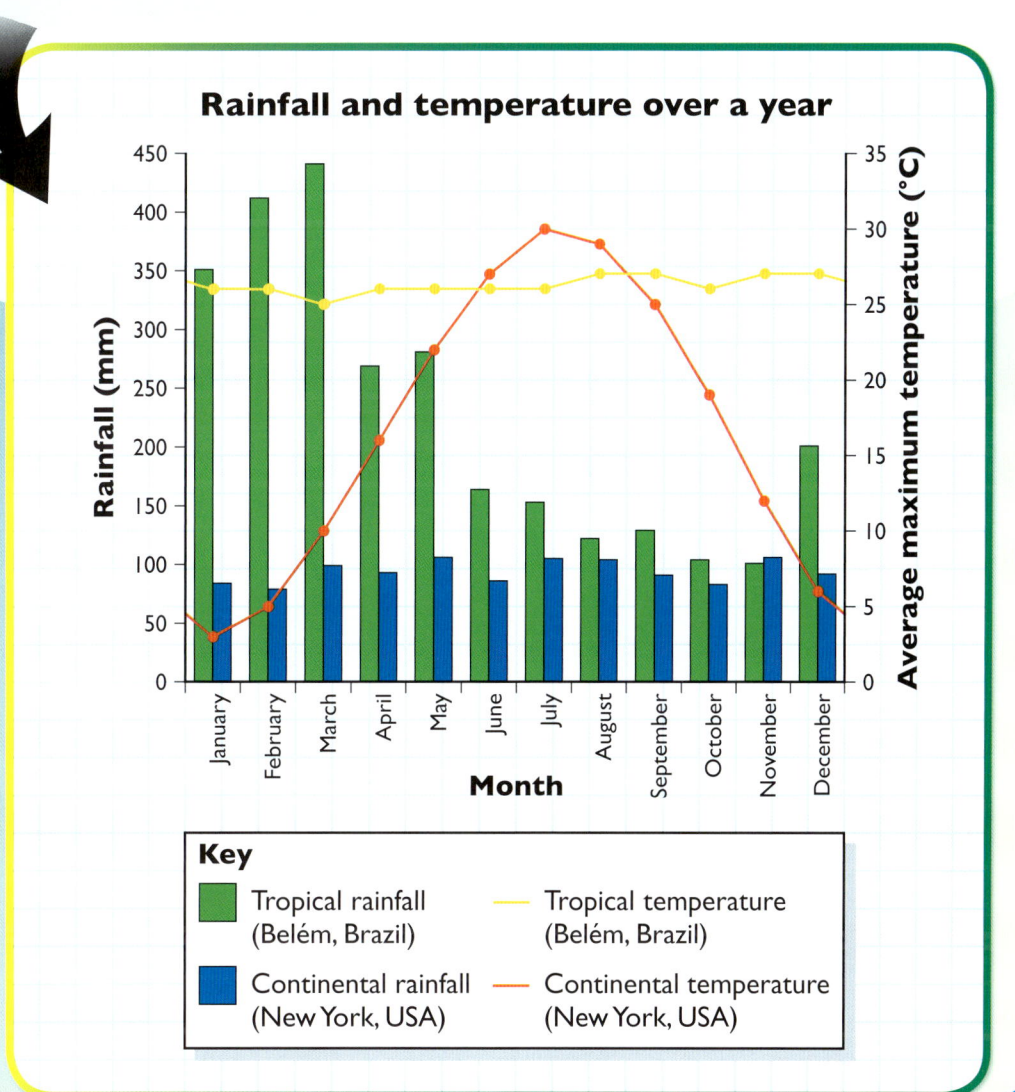

Seasons

Most parts of the world have different weather at different times of the year. For example, in places that have a Mediterranean **climate**, such as Spain, there is hot and dry weather in one part of the year and cool and wet weather in another part of the year. These periods of different weather are called seasons.

 Seasons happen because parts of the Earth are tilted towards or away from the sun as the Earth orbits.

Four seasons

Places that are away from the tropics, towards the Earth's **poles**, normally have four seasons. These seasons are winter, spring, summer, and autumn. Winters are cool or cold, and summers warm or hot. The temperature warms up during spring, and cools down again during autumn. Places such as North America, southern Africa, and northern Europe have four seasons. Places in the tropics do not have four seasons, but often have a rainy season and a dry season.

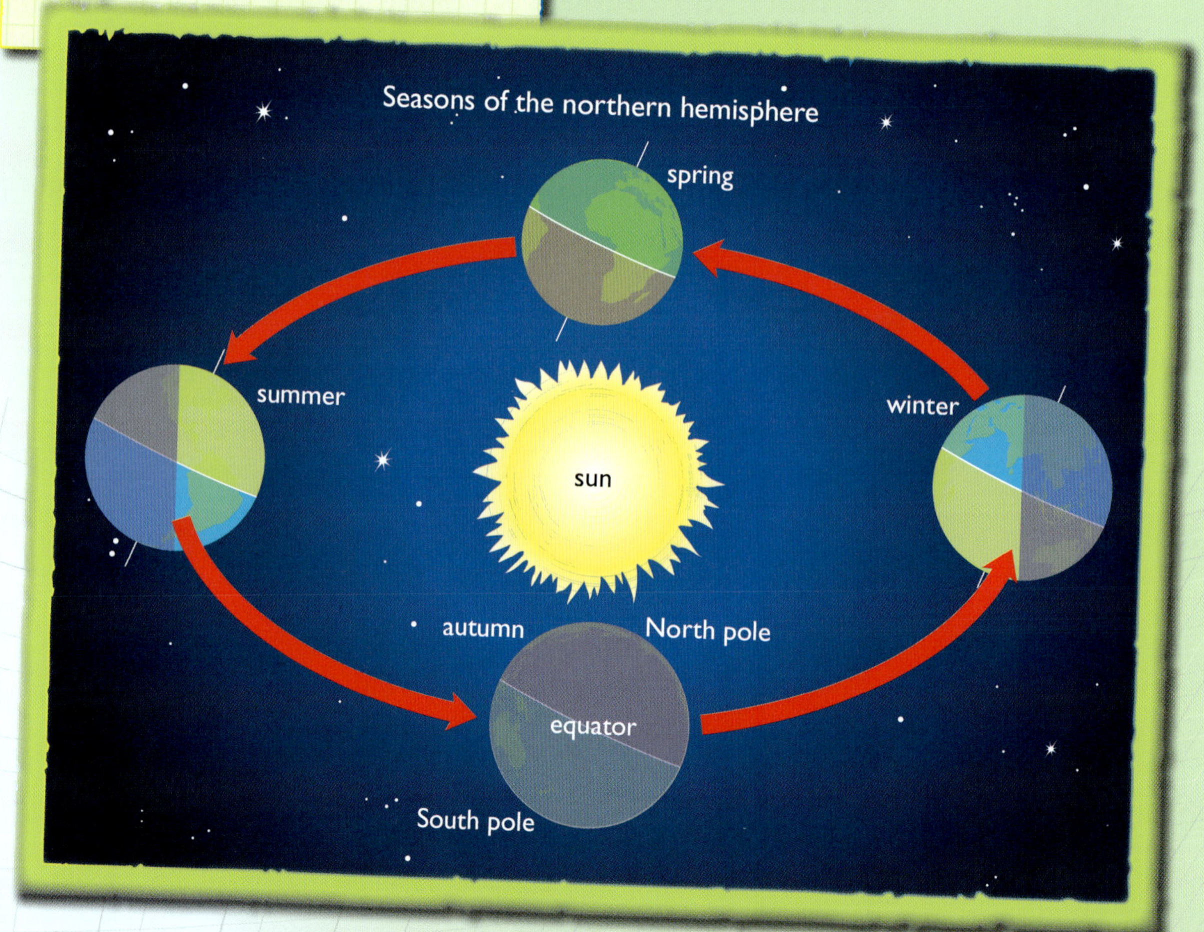

Changing days

The seasons are caused by the tilt of the Earth's **axis**. As the Earth **orbits**, different parts of the world are tilted towards or away from sun. This means they get more or less heat from the sun. For example, when the North Pole and places in the northern hemisphere, such as Europe and North America are tilted towards the sun, they have summer. When they are tilted away from the sun, they have winter.

Daylight hours

In the tropics, it is light for about half the day and dark for about half the day, all year round. Away from the equator near the poles, in summer it is light for longer than it is dark, and in winter, it is dark for longer than it is light. In the Arctic and Antarctic circles, there is no daylight in the mid-winter, and no darkness in the summer.

Double line graphs

This double line graph shows the number of hours of daylight for Seattle, halfway between the **equator** and the North Pole, and for Caracas in Argentina, near the equator. There is one line for each place. Putting both sets of **data** on the same graph makes it easy to compare them.

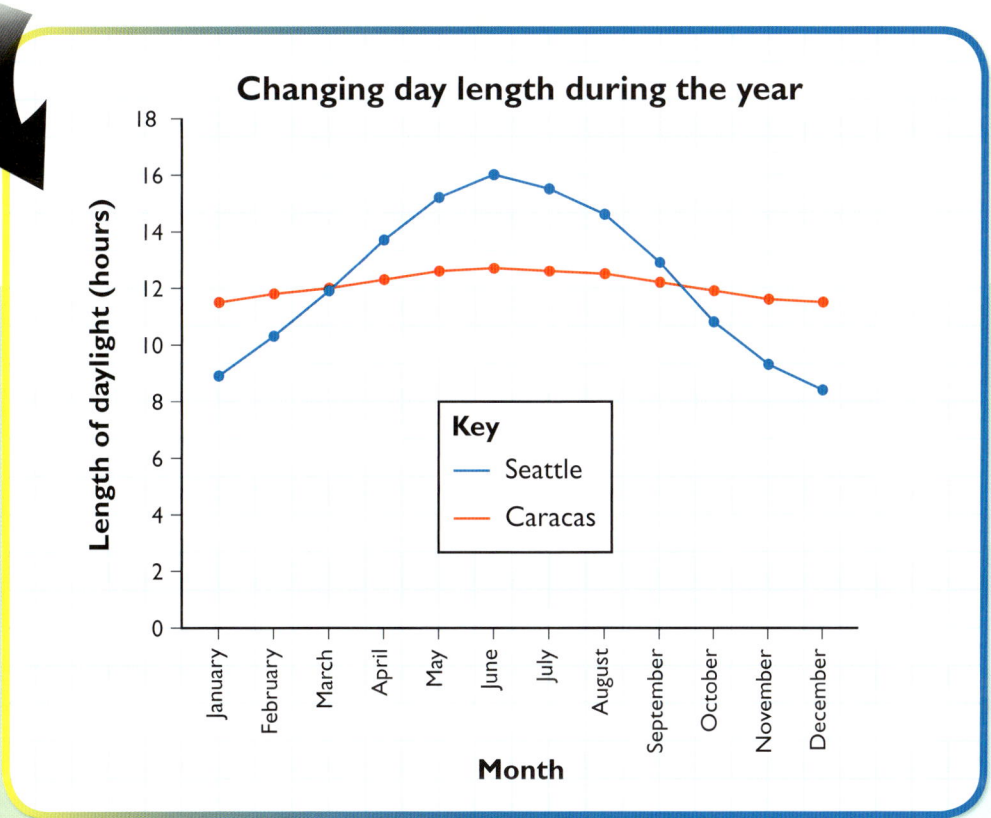

Changing climates

You have probably heard of "**climate change**", but what exactly is it? Simply, it means that climates around the world are slowly changing. They are slightly different today than they were 40 to 60 years ago. Most scientists who study climates agree that climate change is being caused by human activities.

The greenhouse effect and global warming

Earth's **atmosphere** traps heat from the sun. This natural effect is called the **greenhouse effect**. The heat is trapped by some of the gases in the atmosphere, such as carbon dioxide and methane. These gases are called greenhouse gases. Human activities such as burning **fossil fuels** in cars and power stations are adding carbon dioxide and other greenhouse gases to the atmosphere, which means more and more of the sun's heat is being trapped. The temperature of the atmosphere is going up. This is known as **global warming**, and it is causing climate change.

 This graph shows the link between carbon dioxide emissions and the average global temperature.

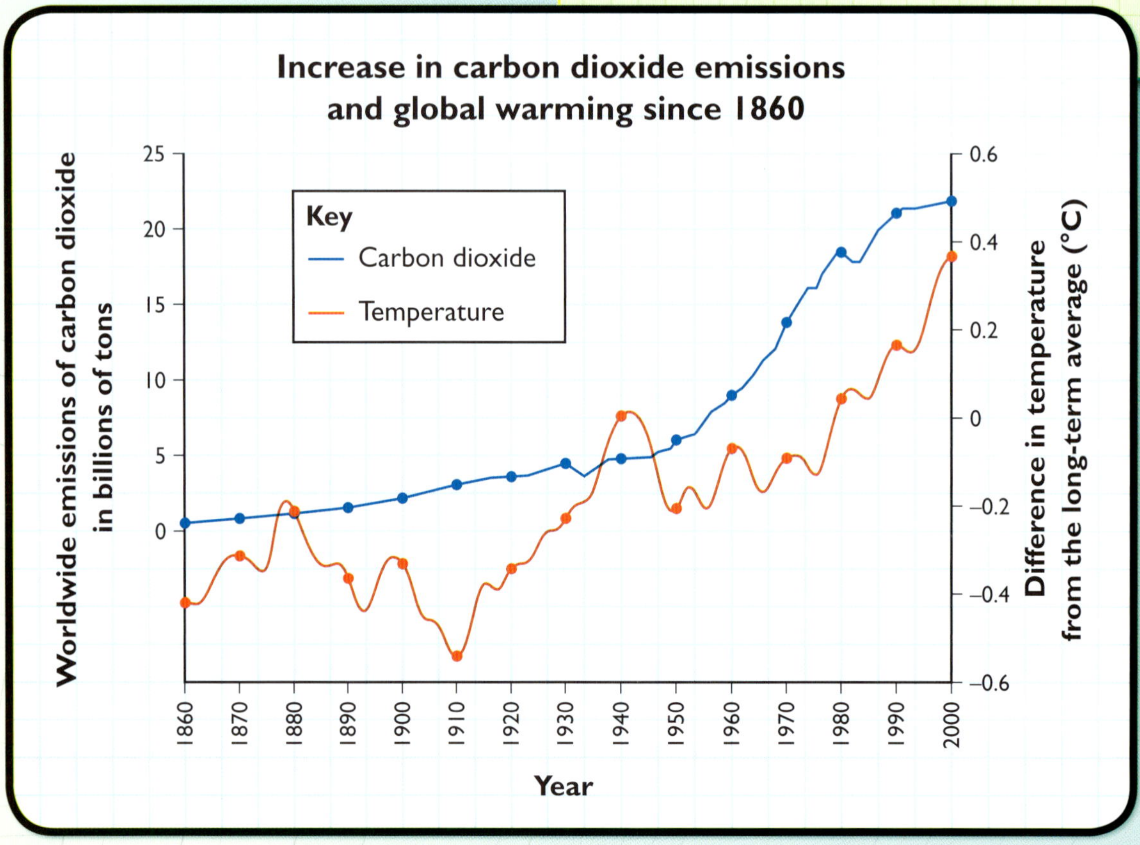

Increase in carbon dioxide emissions and global warming since 1860

 This is a glacier in Alaska, USA. Careful measurements show that many glaciers are getting shorter as temperatures rise.

Evidence for climate change

Weather records for the last few years show that climates are changing. For example, in many places, most recent years have often been hotter on average than before. There are also visible effects of climate change, such as the way rising temperatures are causing polar **ice caps** and **glaciers** to melt.

Climate change in the past

We know that climates have been changing for millions of years. Old weather records, old pictures, and documents show that hundreds of year ago the climate in Europe was colder than today. Ice samples taken from deep under ice caps show us what the temperature was thousands of years ago. Deep valleys in the northern hemisphere show that the area was covered by thick ice 20,000 years ago.

The challenge of climate change

Climate change is one the biggest problems facing the people on Earth. For many of us, it will mean slightly warmer weather all year, with warmer, drier summers and wetter winters. But others will suffer an increase in severe weather events, such as **tropical** storms, extreme winds, heavy rain, or **droughts**. Melting **ice caps** will cause sea levels to rise. This will lead to rises in sea level that will leave many islands and coasts underwater.

Responding to climate change

What can we do about climate change? The first thing we must do is reduce the amount of greenhouse gases we are putting into the **atmosphere**. To achieve this, we must reduce the amount of **fossil fuels** we burn. We can do this by using less energy (for example, by switching off machines we are not using), by using more renewable energy (such as wind energy and solar energy), and by stopping the destruction of rainforests. The governments of many countries agreed to fight climate change at a conference in Bali, Indonesia, in 2007.

We also need to prepare for climate change. For example, people in low-lying coastal areas need to be prepared for more floods. And if climate change does get worse, we will have to adapt to it. For example, in some places we will have to grow different crops, or design new homes to cope with higher temperatures.

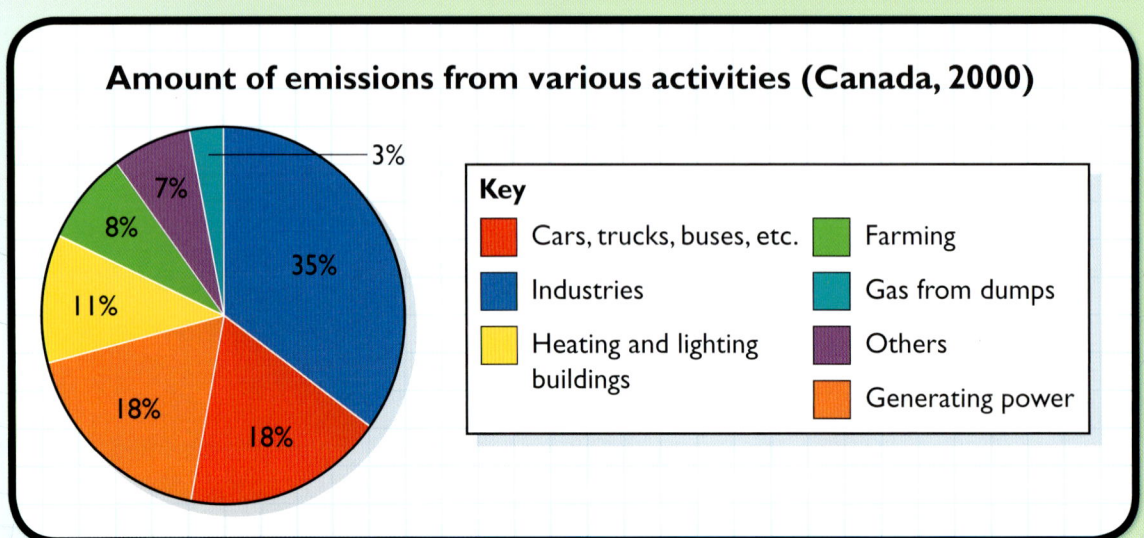

This pie chart shows the different places where carbon emissions come from in Canada.

 Global warming is likely to lead to more **hurricanes**. This is Miami Beach, Florida, USA, during Hurricane Wilma in 2004.

The job of meteorologists

Meteorologists must continue to measure weather and keep weather records to see how climates are changing. The climate **data**, and graphs and charts drawn from it, will tell us how the weather is changing from year to year. The data will also help meteorologists to **forecast** what may happen to Earth's climates in the distant future.

Chart smarts

Data is information about something. We often get important data as a mass of numbers, and it is difficult to make any sense of them. Graphs and charts are ways of displaying information visually. This helps us to see relationships and patterns in the data. Different types of graphs or charts are good for displaying different types of information.

Pictograms

A pictogram shows the amount of something, or how often something happens (its frequency) using pictures.

Cloud cover over an afternoon

Time	Cloud cover
12 noon	☁
1.00 p.m.	☁ ☁ ◖
2.00 p.m.	☁ ☁ ☁ ☁
3.00 p.m.	☁ ☁ ☁ ☁ ◖
4.00 p.m.	☁ ☁ ☁
5.00 p.m.	☁

No cloud cover — Complete cloud cover

Pie charts

A pie chart shows how much of each part of something makes up the whole thing. It is called a pie chart because it looks like a pie cut into pieces.

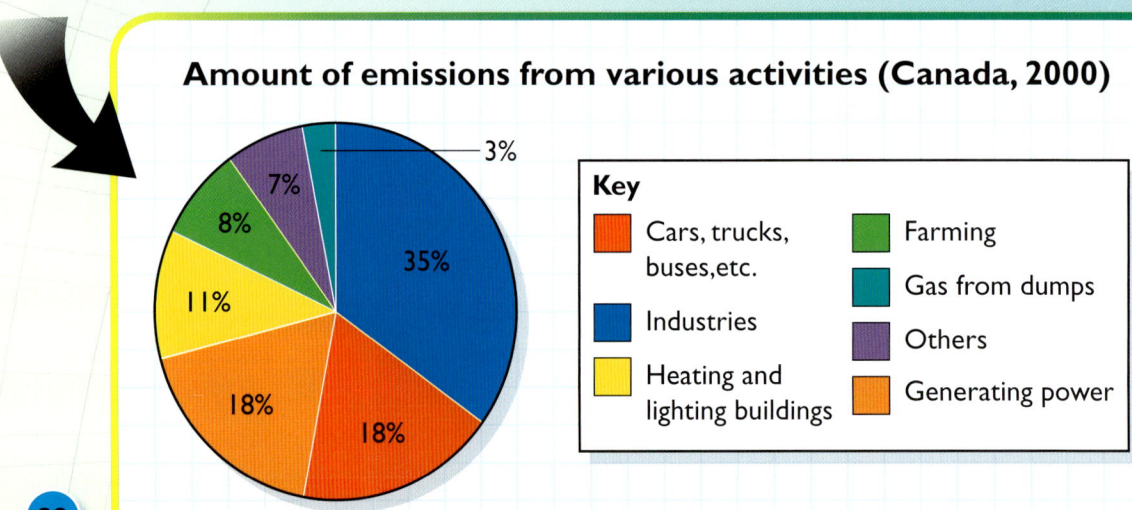

Amount of emissions from various activities (Canada, 2000)

3%, 7%, 8%, 11%, 18%, 18%, 35%

Key:
- Cars, trucks, buses, etc.
- Industries
- Heating and lighting buildings
- Farming
- Gas from dumps
- Others
- Generating power

28

Bar charts

A bar chart (or bar graph) shows the amount of something or how often something happens (its frequency) using bars. The length of a bar shows the amount or frequency. A bar chart can have two of three sets of bars, or bars stacked on top of each other.

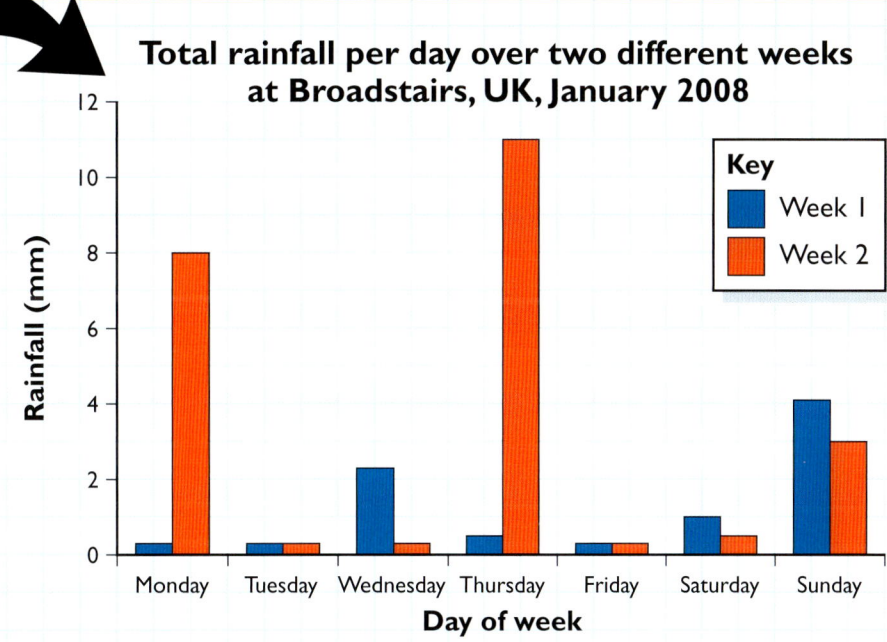

Line graphs

A line graph shows how one thing changes with another, with a line. It shows how the two things are related to each other.

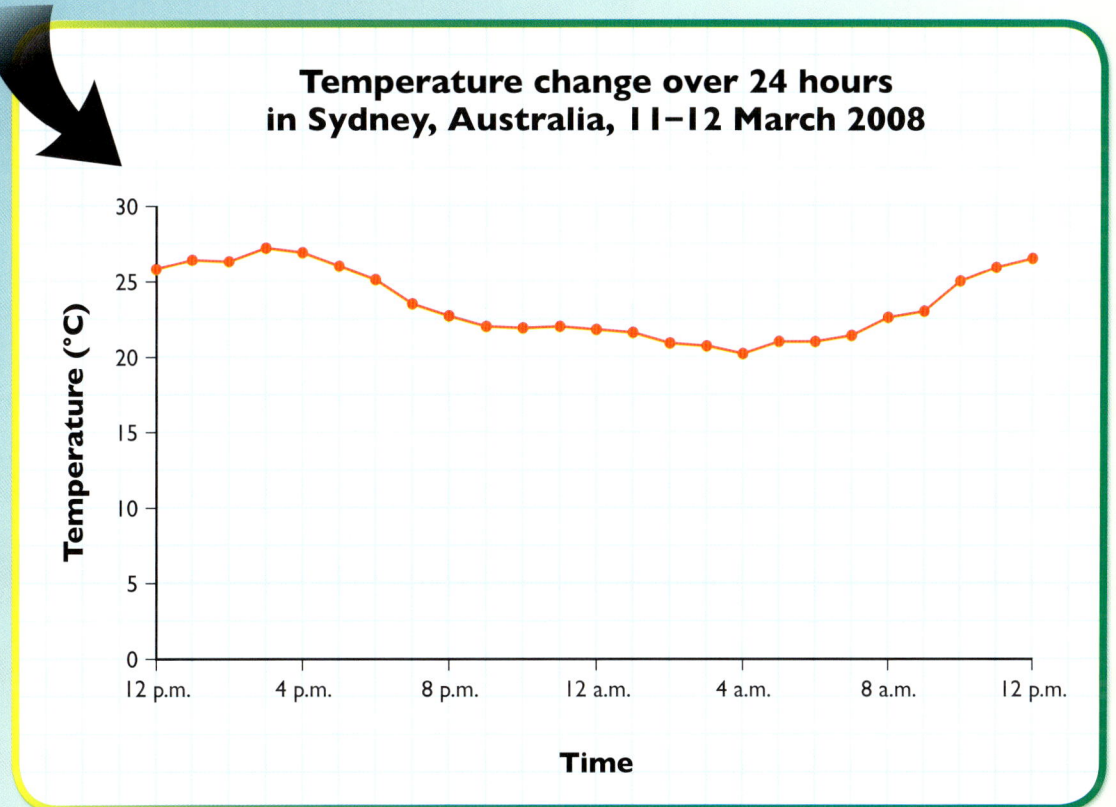

Glossary

atmosphere layer of gases around the Earth

atmospheric pressure push of air in the atmosphere on everything in it

axis imaginary line through the Earth's poles, that the Earth spins round

barometer instrument that measures air pressure

climate pattern of weather at a place over a long period

condensation change in state from liquid to gas

data information, often in the form of numbers

drought long period without rain in place where rain regularly falls

equator imaginary line around the middle of the Earth, an equal distance from the North and South poles

evaporate turn from liquid to gas

forecast predict what will happen

fossil fuel oil, gas, or coal

front boundary between two large air masses with different temperatures

glacier river of ice that moves very slowly down a valley

global warming slight increase in the average temperature of the air in the atmosphere over the last few decades

greenhouse effect way that heat from the sun is trapped by certain gases in the atmosphere, keeping the air in the atmosphere warm

humidity measure of the amount of water vapour in the air

hurricane intense swirling weather system that forms over the Atlantic Ocean, bringing very strong winds and heavy rainfall

hygrometer instrument for measuring humidity

ice cap deep sheet of ice covering land

meteorologist scientist who studies weather and climate

millibar unit of pressure, equal to 0.1 kilopascals

orbit the path that an object in space takes around another object in space. For example, the Earth orbits the sun.

pole place where the Earth's axis meets the surface of the Earth (the North Pole and the South Pole)

precipitation any water or ice that falls from the atmosphere to the ground (rain, snow, or hail)

radar device that uses radio waves to detect objects in the air. Weather radars can detect rainfall in the air.

satellite any object, natural or manufactured, that orbits a planet

storm surge rise in sea level caused by the low pressure under a tropical storm, which can cause coastal flooding

temperate describes a climate without very hot or very cold weather

tornado spinning funnel of air that descends from a storm cloud

transpiration when water from the leaves of a plant evaporates into the air

tropical to do with the narrow band of land and sea on each side of the equator

water cycle the circulation of water between the oceans, the atmosphere, the land, and rivers

water vapour gas form of water

x-axis horizontal line on a graph

y-axis vertical line on a graph

Further information

Books

Global Warming (Our Planet in Peril series), Chris Oxlade (Franklin Watts, 2002)

How the Weather Works, Michael Allaby (Dorling Kindersley, 1995)

Storm Warning: Tornadoes (Turbulent Planet series), Chris Oxlade (Raintree, 2005)

Violent Skies: Hurricanes (Turbulent Planet series), Chris Oxlade (Raintree, 2005)

Websites

This website allows you to create almost any sort of graph from your own data! nces.ed.gov/nceskids/createagraph/default.aspx

The BBC skillswise website has factsheets on different types of charts and graphs, and worksheets to try. www.bbc.co.uk/skillswise/numbers/handlingdata/graphs_and_charts/

Visit the Australian Bureau of Meteorology website to find out what the weather is like in different parts of Australia. By clicking on "Learn about meteorology" and then "Weather education" you can learn about weather and climate and find links to other useful sites. www.bom.gov.au

This website for the Meteorological Office in the United Kingdom has lots of information about the weather, including data and graphs about recent weather. www.metoffice.co.uk

The National Oceanic and Atmospheric Administration in the United States has information about the weather and climates, plus some free weather data. www.noaa.gov

Index

air masses 14, 15
anemometers 8
atmosphere 6–7, 11, 12, 14, 24, 26
atmospheric pressure 6, 7, 8, 9

barometers 6, 16

carbon emissions 24, 26
climate change 24–7
climates 5, 20–1, 22
    microclimates 21
    temperate climate 20, 21
    tropical climate 20, 21
clouds 10–11, 12, 15

data 5, 13, 17, 20, 23, 27, 28
day length 23
droughts 18, 26

extreme weather 17, 18–19

floods 17, 18, 19, 26
forecasts 5, 16–17, 27

global warming 24, 25, 27
graphs and charts 5
    bar charts 5, 9, 13, 16, 19, 21, 29
    double bar charts 13
    double line graphs 23
    keys 13
    line graphs 7, 21, 23, 24, 29
    pictograms 11, 28
    pie charts 26, 28
    x-axis 7
    y-axis 7
greenhouse gases 24, 26

hail 12, 18
heatwaves 18
humidity 10, 20
hurricanes 19, 27
hygrometers 10

meterologists 5, 8, 11, 14, 16, 20, 27

precipitation 12, 20

rain gauges 13, 16
rainfall 12, 13, 15, 17, 18, 20, 21, 26

seasons 22–3
severe weather warnings 17
snow 12, 15, 16, 17, 18

temperatures 7, 9, 18, 21, 22, 24, 25
thermometers 7, 16
thunder clouds 11, 12, 19
tornadoes 17, 19
tropical cyclones 19

water cycle 12
water vapour 6, 10, 14
weather 5
weather fronts 14–15
    cold fronts 14, 15
    warm fronts 14
weather systems
    high-pressure 15, 17
    low-pressure 15, 17
wind vanes 8
winds 8–9, 15, 17, 18, 19, 26
    global winds 9
    local winds 8
    speed and direction 8, 9, 19